the guide to owning a
Tonkinese Cat

Lorraine Shelton

Photo: Isabelle Francais

© T.F.H. Publications, Inc.

Distributed in the UNITED STATES to the Pet Trade by T.F.H. Publications, Inc., 1 TFH Plaza, Neptune City, NJ 07753; on the Internet at www.tfh.com; in CANADA by Rolf C. Hagen Inc., 3225 Sartelon St., Montreal, Quebec H4R 1E8; Pet Trade by H & L Pet Supplies Inc., 27 Kingston Crescent, Kitchener, Ontario N2B 2T6; in ENGLAND by T.F.H. Publications, PO Box 74, Havant PO9 5TT; in AUSTRALIA AND THE SOUTH PACIFIC by T.F.H. (Australia), Pty. Ltd., Box 149, Brookvale 2100 N.S.W., Australia; in NEW ZEALAND by Brooklands Aquarium Ltd., 5 McGiven Drive, New Plymouth, RD1 New Zealand; in SOUTH AFRICA by Rolf C. Hagen S.A. (PTY.) LTD., P.O. Box 201199, Durban North 4016, South Africa; in JAPAN by T.F.H. Publications. Published by T.F.H. Publications, Inc.

**MANUFACTURED IN THE
UNITED STATES OF AMERICA
BY T.F.H. PUBLICATIONS, INC.**

Contents

The publisher thanks the following owners of cats pictured in this book: Mark Campbell, David and Laurie Holmes, Carol and Roland Mackay, Geslot Mepanie, Mary Mosshammer, Debra Raynor, Ruth and Fred Riley, Jill Selkowitz, June Shatto, Bonnie L. Smith, Deborah Stewart-Parker, Barbara Swanson, Janice Van Wold, Karen White, Carol Decker White, and the members of the Tonkinese Breeders Association.

Photo: Isabelle Francais

Introduction to the Tonkinese Cat

A silky, mink-like coat covering a muscular body, an intriguing variety of colors, a playful personality, and entrancing aqua eyes are among the hallmarks of the beautiful cat known as the Tonkinese. Combining the grace, intelligence, curiosity, and elegance of the Siamese with the powerful body, laid-back personality, and rounded features of the Burmese, the Tonkinese is the "happy medium" cat, with a personality as pleasing as its appearance.

Although the Burmese and Siamese breeds were once similar in body type, the exhibition Siamese cat has been selectively bred into an extreme expression of length and slimness, while the Burmese has evolved

The Tonkinese is the "happy medium" between the Siamese and Burmese breeds, with a personality as pleasing as its appearance. *Photo: Isabelle Francais*

Although Tonkinese cats are active and playful, they are not high-strung. *Photo: Isabelle Francais*

in the opposite direction, especially in the United States, to become a stocky and short-muzzled breed of cat. Cat lovers with a memory of the "apple-headed," Siamese-colored cats that they or other family members have owned in the past will be delighted to learn that a beautiful breed of cat exists that embodies that vision but takes it to new heights of feline beauty. Although the Tonkinese cat represents the best of both the Siamese and Burmese worlds through its distant ancestors, it is a unique and separate breed. Since its beginnings as a breed in the 1960s, the Tonkinese has won its way into many cat-loving hearts, becoming one of the ten most popular breeds in the cat fancy.

PERSONALITY

Once you've brought a Tonkinese into your family, your life will never be the same.

Your Tonkinese will become more than just a pet. She will be a friendly companion, a warm addition to your bed, and a purring shoulder adornment, and she will lend a curious paw to almost everything you do around the house. Friendly and tolerant, a Tonkinese can be a wonderful choice for households with older children or other pets. Although they are active and muscular, they are not high-strung. This breed has excelled at being feline ambassadors, bringing special joy to those in nursing homes or hospitals. The Tonkinese is an intelligent, gregarious, happy cat with a sense of humor. Tonkinese cats do like to talk, but with a bit less enthusiasm and insistence and with a more mellow voice than their Siamese ancestors. Do not consider bringing home a Tonkinese unless you have time in your life for games like fetch and hide-and-seek. Tonks know the meaning of fun!

Do not consider bringing home a Tonkinese unless you have time for plenty of games. Tonks know the meaning of fun! *Photo: Isabelle Francais*

History of the Tonkinese Cat

Although the Tonkinese breed is relatively new to the cat fancy, the combination of the graceful Siamese and the powerful Burmese has existed for centuries in the Orient. Long before the name "Tonkinese" was used to describe them, these cats were

The graceful Siamese breed's body type has been modified over the years so that it is no longer identical to that of the Tonkinese.
Photo: Isabelle Francais

represented in *The Cat-Book Poems of Siam*, written during the Ayudha Period (1358–1767). When Tonkinese cats were first imported to England in the early 1800s, they were called "Chocolate Siamese" or "Golden Siamese." Other names attributed to them throughout the centuries include "Si-Burm," "Zibeline," and "Golden Chechong."

Both the Tonkinese and Burmese breeds in the US trace their pedigrees back to Wong Mau, a small, walnut-colored cat brought to California by Dr. Joseph Thompson in 1930. Because there were no other cats like her in the country, she was mated with a Siamese. Half of the kittens produced from this breeding were Siamese-colored, "pointed" kittens, and half were walnut-colored kittens like Wong Mau herself. When one of these brown kittens was mated back to his mother, the surprising result was that three distinct types of kittens were produced: pointed kittens with blue eyes, kittens the color of their mother with greenish to aqua-colored eyes, and darker brown kittens with yellowish-green to golden eyes. The darker kittens would prove to breed true to color and became the foundation of the Burmese breed. Admirers of Wong Mau herself had to wait two more decades before different breeders in different parts of the world again began to experiment with those aqua-eyed "in-between" cats that were not quite Siamese and not quite Burmese.

In the 1950s, a pet store owner in New York City named Milan Greer began breeding "Golden Siamese," a hybrid of his own pet Siamese and Burmese. These cats were an attractive blending of the two breeds, with a body that was tan to brown and a mask, ears, legs, and tail ("points") that were seal brown or almost black. Greer's cats were enormously popular with

Darker kittens resulting from the same breedings that created the Tonkinese became the foundation of the Burmese breed. *Photo: Isabelle Francais*

Tonkinese cats have existed for centuries under many names, including Chocolate Siamese, Golden Siamese, Si-Burm, Zibeline, and Golden Chechong. *Photo: Isabelle Francais*

In the mid-1960s, the Tonkinese breed, with its mink-colored fur and beautiful aqua eyes, was firmly established for the first time. *Photo: Karen White*

pet buyers in New York City during the 1950s and early 1960s, but his cats did not become the ancestors of the Tonkinese breed of today.

In the mid-1960s, Jane Barletta in New Jersey and Margaret Conroy in Canada independently launched other breeding programs, producing Siamese/Burmese hybrids of their own. The color of these brown cats with darker points was called "natural mink," because their breeders felt that the fur resembled natural, undyed mink. The new breed was named Tonkinese and was first accepted for championship status by the Canadian Cat Association (CCA) in 1971. Tonkinese cats have since been accepted by all cat registries in the US and by many other registry associations in countries throughout the world.

In the early years of this breed, crosses to blue and chocolate point Siamese, as well as to champagne (also called chocolate) Burmese, expanded the Tonkinese spectrum. The breed was established in four colors, with three varieties each. The colors are *natural* (also called brown or seal), *blue, champagne* (also called chocolate), and *platinum* (also called lilac or frost). The three varieties that each color can be expressed as are *pointed* (Siamese-patterned), *mink* (also called intermediate or "light-phase Burmese"), and *solid* (also called sepia or "dark-phase Burmese"). Different cat registries refer to these colors by different names. Some associations only accept the aqua-eyed, mink colors for competition, while other associations accept all three varieties of each color for competition. For simplicity's sake, the color conventions of the world's largest cat registry, the Cat Fanciers' Association

(CFA), will be used throughout this book. In the CFA, the three accepted varieties are solid, mink, and pointed, and the four colors are natural, champagne, blue, and platinum.

A fifth color existed in the early years of the Tonkinese, called "honey." This color is related to the cinnamon color found in Oriental, Abyssinian, and Somali cats. Unfortunately, a health problem appeared to be more common in cats from this line, and breeding of cats in this color was eventually discontinued.

Until 1984, Tonkinese were allowed to be bred to both Siamese and Burmese to establish a broad gene pool. In 1984, outcrosses to other breeds were disallowed, and ever since, Tonkinese are only bred to other Tonkinese. A unique body and head type was established through selective breeding. Even though some Tonkinese may share the color of a Burmese or Siamese, there is no mistaking that they are Tonks through and through.

Crosses to blue and chocolate point Siamese expanded the palette of the Tonkinese breed. New colors were developed, such as these kittens' platinum coats. *Photo: Isabelle Francais*

Standard and Colors of the Tonkinese

Every Tonkinese is a beautiful example of a unique member of the feline species. These cats come in a variety of spectacular colors, caused by a series of genetic phenomena. How do breeders decide which kitten in a litter to keep to best further the breed? And how can a judge decide which Tonkinese in a large group of cats or kittens to award with cat show prizes? The key lies in a written description of the perfect cat of each breed, called a standard of excellence (or "standard" for short). In this document, the founders of the breed and

By comparing each kitten to the breed standard, experienced breeders decide which of their Tonkinese have show potential. *Photo: Karen White*

the fanciers that follow describe the colors and conformation of a Tonkinese cat in the most precise terms possible. They paint a picture with words of the structural and aesthetic qualities that they believe epitomize the breed. This allows someone to look at different cats of a breed and determine which one is the best example of that breed and, perhaps, which is destined to become a top show winner or a valuable breeding animal. Every year, expert breeders evaluate the written standard to ensure that it provides proper guidance to those who are working with the breed.

THE COLORS

Differences between some of the Tonkinese colors and varieties can be subtle. Breeders and judges need to develop a skilled and experienced eye

Cat show judges and Tonkinese breeders must develop a skilled and experienced eye before they are able to recognize the breed's various colors and varieties. *Photo: Lorraine Shelton*

In the cooler parts of a pointed or mink Tonkinese cat's body, such as the nose, feet, and tail, a heat-sensitive enzyme produces a darker fur color. *Photo: Isabelle Francais*

Because newborn Tonkinese are warm all over from their mother's body, they are born very light and even in color. *Photo: Isabelle Francais*

before they are able to classify the colors correctly. Paw pad color is the easiest way to distinguish among the four basic colors, and eye color can be used as a clue to variety, especially in the lighter colors where the difference between body color and point color can be less distinct. As any Tonkinese gets older, the body color will darken, with breeding males showing the greatest degree of change.

The Tonkinese varieties are a result of the actions of a heat-sensitive enzyme that is essential to the chemical reaction that creates color in the skin and hair of the cat. The pointed colors have the most temperature-sensitive form of this enzyme. In the warmest part of a pointed cat's body,

this enzyme doesn't work at all, creating an almost white torso. In the cooler parts of the body, called the "points" (the nose, feet, and tail), the enzyme works well and color is produced. In the mink variety, the enzyme is less sensitive, and the difference between point and body color is not as prominent as in the pointed variety. In the solid (or sepia) variety, the enzyme is only slightly affected by temperature, and the points and body are almost the same color.

In warmer climates or homes, a Tonkinese may become lighter in color. In a colder environment, the cat may become darker. A cat that has a habit of lying on a floor heating vent, for example, will have a light-colored belly. A newborn Tonkinese is warm all over from the heat of his mother's body. This is why a Tonkinese kitten is born very light and even in color. The cooler temperature of the kitten's new world will cause him to darken in shade as he grows. As the cat becomes older, his body and skin temperatures decrease slightly, resulting in his color darkening with maturity and even more as he approaches his senior years.

In the mink variety, the most unique color phase of this breed, the coat color is lighter than the point color, creating a definite distinction between the body color and the points. These cats have a characteristic aqua eye color. Body color in solid (also called sepia) Tonkinese is a slightly lighter shade of the point color, providing very little contrast with the points. The lighter colors tend to show more contrast between body and point color than the darker colors. The eye color may be any shade from green to gold. The pointed Tonkinese has a light body color, anywhere from stark white to deep cream, that is in dramatic contrast to the point color. The eyes are blue.

Natural or Seal

The natural mink (also called seal mink) Tonkinese has a medium-brown body, sometimes with ruddy highlights. The natural solid (also called sable sepia) has a sable, deep-brown body. The natural point or seal point has a body that is fawn to cream. In all varieties of this color, the points and nose leather are dark brown and the paw pads are a medium to dark brown, sometimes with a rosy undertone.

Chocolate or Champagne

The chocolate or champagne mink Tonkinese has a body that is buff-cream to beige. Reddish highlights are acceptable in show cats. The chocolate sepia (or solid) champagne has a body that is golden-tan to light coffee-brown in color. The champagne or chocolate point has a body that is ivory with buff-tan shading. In all varieties of this color, the points are a medium-brown color. The nose leather is cinnamon-brown and the paw pads are cinnamon-pink to cinnamon-brown.

Blue

The blue mink Tonkinese is a soft, blue-gray color with warm overtones. The shade

The natural mink Tonkinese has a medium-brown body and dark-brown points.
Photo: Isabelle Francais

The champagne solid Tonkinese has a golden-tan to light coffee-brown body with slightly darker points. *Photo: Isabelle Francais*

may range from light to medium blue. The solid or sepia blue Tonkinese has a body that is slate blue with warm overtones. The blue point Tonkinese has an off-white body with warm gray shading. In each variety of blue Tonkinese, the points are slate blue and are distinctly darker than the body color. The nose leather is blue-gray and the paw pads are blue-gray, sometimes with a rosy undertone.

Lilac or Platinum
The lilac or platinum mink Tonkinese has a pale, silvery gray body with warm overtones. The color must not be white or cream, but rather a pale lavender. The platinum solid or lilac sepia has a body that is dove gray. The

platinum or lilac point Tonkinese has a body that is pearly white. The points, in all varieties, are frosty gray. The nose leather is lavender-pink to lavender-gray, and the paw pads are a slightly lavender-washed shade of pink.

THE STANDARD
Tonkinese breeders, working together, strive to produce the perfect example of their breed. In order to achieve this, breeders must share a common language and a common vision. The written standard describes perfection in a breed and provides a point structure by which individual cats can be compared to that standard of excellence, both by judges in the show ring and by other breeders in developing their own breeding programs. The features that the breeders have decided are most important in their breed will receive a greater allocation of these points than a feature that is not considered as important in defining the breed. The standard reprinted here is the one used by breeders registering in the Cat Fanciers' Association (CFA). The author's comments and explanations of some of the more difficult terms follow some sections in italics.

POINT SCORE
Head (25)

Profile 8

Muzzle and chin 6

Ears 6

Eye shape and set 5

Body (30)

Torso 15

Legs and feet 5

Tail 5

GENERAL

The ideal Tonkinese is intermediate in type, neither cobby nor svelte. The Tonkinese should give the overall impression of an alert, active cat with good muscular development. The cat should be surprisingly heavy. While the breed is considered medium in size, balance and proportion are of greater importance.

Head and Muzzle

The head is a modified slightly rounded wedge somewhat longer than it is wide, with high gently planed cheekbones. The muzzle is blunt, as long as it is wide. There is a slight whisker break, gently curved, following the lines of the wedge. There is a slight stop at eye level. In profile the tip of the chin lines with the tip of the nose in the same vertical plane. There is a gentle rise from the tip of the nose to the stop. There is a gentle contour with a slight rise from the nose stop to the forehead. There is a slight convex curve to the forehead.

Author's Comments: The muzzle is the part of the head around the nose. A slight break in the lines of the wedge in back of the whisker pads, defining the muzzle, is called a whisker break. The head, in profile, exhibits a slight curved indentation at the level of the eyes (called a "stop").

Ears

Alert, medium in size. Oval tips, broad at the base. Ears set as much on the sides of the head as on the top. Hair on the ears very short and close-lying. Leather may show through.

Author's Comments: The fur on the ears is very short; because of this, the skin underneath may show through. The ears should actually appear to be pricked forward, rather than standing straight up. The space between the ears should be approximately 1 to 1 $^1/_2$ times the width of an ear.

A platinum mink Tonkinese like GC Kipkat Venus Prime of B4 Kipkat has a pale, silvery gray body with warm overtones and frosty gray points.
Photo: Isabelle Francais

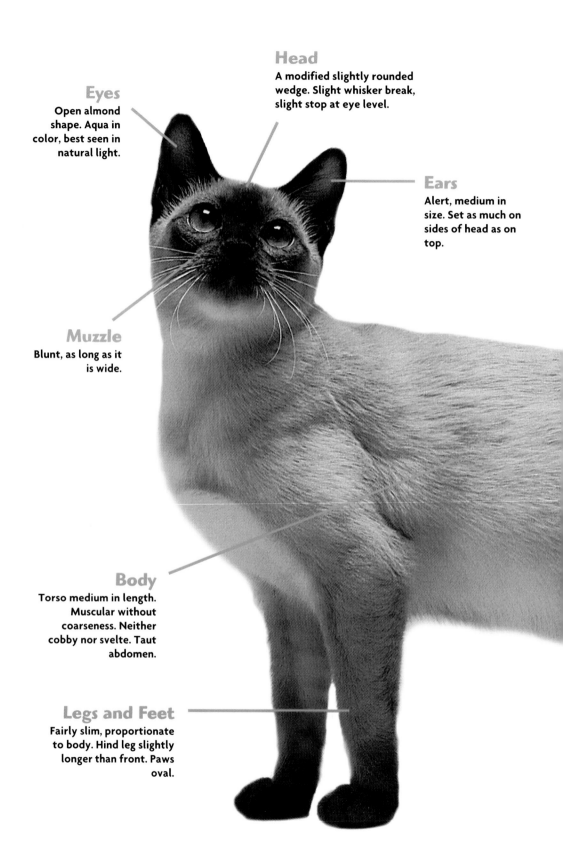

Head
A modified slightly rounded wedge. Slight whisker break, slight stop at eye level.

Eyes
Open almond shape. Aqua in color, best seen in natural light.

Ears
Alert, medium in size. Set as much on sides of head as on top.

Muzzle
Blunt, as long as it is wide.

Body
Torso medium in length. Muscular without coarseness. Neither cobby nor svelte. Taut abdomen.

Legs and Feet
Fairly slim, proportionate to body. Hind leg slightly longer than front. Paws oval.

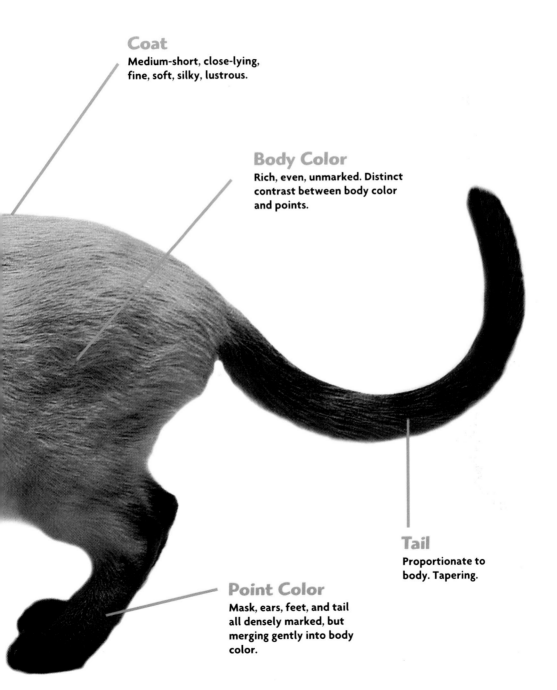

Coat
Medium-short, close-lying, fine, soft, silky, lustrous.

Body Color
Rich, even, unmarked. Distinct contrast between body color and points.

Tail
Proportionate to body. Tapering.

Point Color
Mask, ears, feet, and tail all densely marked, but merging gently into body color.

The muzzle of a Tonkinese should be blunt, and the head should be a modified, slightly rounded wedge somewhat longer than it is wide, with high, gently planed cheekbones. *Photo: Isabelle Francais*

challenge to judges, as the shade may change appearance based on different types of lighting. Eye color is best judged under natural lighting, and many a judge has taken a Tonkinese cat away from the judging table to a nearby window in order to evaluate the eye color. Eye color can change with age, hormonal surges, and sexual maturity.

Eyes

Open almond shape. Slanted along the cheekbones toward the outer edge of the ear. Eyes are proportionate in size to the face.

Eye Color

Aqua. A definitive characteristic of the Tonkinese breed, best seen in natural light. Depth, clarity, and brilliance of color preferred.

Author's Comments: The eye color must be aqua (keep in mind that in CFA only the mink colors may be shown). Tonkinese breeders see eye color as a defining characteristic of their breed and assign a full ten points to this feature alone. Depth, clarity, and brilliance of color are highly prized. Eye color can present a

Body

Torso medium in length, demonstrating well-developed muscular strength without coarseness. The Tonkinese conformation strikes a midpoint between the extremes of long, svelte body types and cobby, compact body types. Balance and proportion are more important than size alone. The abdomen should be taut, well-muscled, and firm.

Author's Comments: The cat should have well-developed muscles but should not appear bulky or coarse. The abdomen should be firm and well muscled, without loose skin. The ribcage should be rounded.

Legs and Feet

Fairly slim, proportionate in length and bone to the body. Hind legs slightly longer than front. Paws more oval than round. Trim. Toes: five in front and four behind.

Author's Comments: A large male may have heavier boning than a petite female. The hind legs should be slightly longer than front legs, providing for powerful jumping ability, but neither should be so long as to appear out of balance with the rest of the body.

Tail

Proportionate in length to body. Tapering.

Coat

Medium short in length, close-lying, fine, soft and silky, with a lustrous sheen.

Author's Comments: Tonkinese fur is medium short in length and lies close to the skin. Its texture should be reminiscent of a fine mink. The coat should never feel coarse or dry.

Body Color

The mature specimen should be a rich, even, unmarked color, shading almost imperceptibly to a slightly lighter hue on the underparts. Allowance to be made for lighter body color in young cats. With the dilute colors in particular, development of full body color may take up to 16 months. Cats do darken with age, but there must be a distinct contrast between body color and points.

Point Color

Mask, ears, feet, and tail all densely marked, but merging gently into body color. Except in kittens, mask and ears should be connected by tracings.

Author's Comments: Tracings are markings containing the dense color of the points.

Penalize

Extreme ranginess or cobbiness. Definite nose break. Round eyes.

Author's Comments: The judge should remove points from a Tonkinese's score if the cat exhibits ranginess or cobbiness, flaws in overall body size and shape. Also, if the nose stop is so exaggerated as to be a sharp change in direction, then the cat must be penalized. A judge must also take away points for round eyes.

Disqualify

Yellow eyes. White locket or button. Crossed eyes. Tail faults.

Author's Comments: A judge must disqualify from competition any Tonkinese that has yellow eyes. The coat must be free of small white areas in the fur. Crossed eyes are considered a serious fault, because it took many generations of selective breeding to eliminate this trait from the Tonkinese's Siamese ancestors. There must be no kinks or abnormalities in the tail. As with all breeds, whole males must have both testicles descended and all cats must have all body parts present and functioning normally.

GC, RW Vanwin Forevr Krystal of Karessence, a champagne mink, pictured here at four months of age. *Photo: Karen White*

TONKINESE COLORS

Natural Mink
Body: medium brown. Ruddy highlights acceptable. *Points:* dark brown. *Nose leather:* dark brown (corresponding to the intensity of the point color). *Paw pads:* medium to dark brown (may have a rosy undertone).

Champagne Mink
Body: buff-cream to beige. Reddish highlights acceptable. *Points:* medium brown. *Nose leather:* cinnamon-brown (corresponding to the intensity of the point color). *Paw pads:* cinnamon-pink to cinnamon-brown.

Blue Mink
Body: soft, blue-gray with warm overtones. *Points:* slate blue, distinctly darker than the body color. *Nose leather:* blue-gray (corresponding to the intensity of the point color). *Paw pads:* blue-gray (may have a rosy undertone).

Platinum Mink
Body: pale, silvery gray with warm overtones. Not white or cream. *Points:* frosty gray, distinctly darker than the body color. *Nose leather:* lavender-pink to lavender-gray. *Paw pads:* lavender-pink.

ANY OTHER VARIETY (AOV) COLOR STANDARDS

General Description—
Solid Colors (AOV)
Body color in solid AOVs may be a slightly lighter shade of the point color, with very little contrast with points. There will be more contrast between points and body color for the Champagne and Platinum solid than for the Natural and Blue solids. *Eye color:* green to yellow/green.

Natural Solid (AOV): *Body:* sable brown. *Points:* dark brown. *Nose leather:* dark brown (corresponding to the intensity of the point color). *Paw pads:* medium to dark brown (may have a rosy undertone).

Champagne Solid (AOV): *Body:* golden tan to light coffee brown. *Points:* medium brown. *Nose leather:* cinnamon-brown (corresponding to the intensity of the point color). *Paw pads:* cinnamon-pink to cinnamon-brown.

Blue Solid (AOV): *Body:* slate blue with warm overtones. *Points:* slate blue. *Nose leather:* blue-gray (corresponding to the intensity of the point color). *Paw pads:* blue-gray (may have a rosy undertone).

Platinum Solid (AOV): *Body:* dove gray. *Points:* frosty gray. *Nose leather:* lavender-pink to lavender-gray. *Paw pads:* lavender-pink.

General Description—
Pointed Colors (AOV)
Body color in pointed AOVs should be off-white, any shading relative to the point color; overall body color should be in marked contrast to the points. *Eye color:* blue.

Natural Point (AOV): *Body:* fawn to cream. *Points:* dark brown. *Nose leather:* dark brown (corresponding to the intensity of the point color). *Paw pads:* medium to dark brown (may have a rosy undertone).

No matter how closely your Tonkinese conforms to the breed standard, he or she will make a wonderful friend and companion. *Photo: Isabelle Francais*

Champagne Point (AOV): *Body:* ivory with buff-tan shading. *Points:* medium brown. *Nose leather:* cinnamon-brown (corresponding to the intensity of the point color). *Paw pads:* cinnamon-pink to cinnamon-brown.

Blue Point (AOV): *Body:* off-white with warm gray shading. *Points:* slate blue. *Nose leather:* blue-gray (corresponding to the intensity of the point color). *Paw pads:* blue-gray (may have a rosy undertone).

Platinum Point (AOV): *Body:* pearly white. *Points:* frosty-gray. *Nose leather:* lavender-pink to lavender-gray (corresponding to the intensity of the point color). *Paw pads:* lavender-pink.

* Tonkinese allowable outcross breeds: none.

Selecting a Tonkinese Cat

When your search begins for a Tonkinese, you may find that these cats are fairly rare and difficult to find, depending on where you live. Cat shows, magazines, referrals from the cat registries, and the Internet can be excellent resources for locating the right cat for you. Breeders are very particular about the type of home they want for their precious babies. Prepare to develop a relationship with the breeder of your kitten. As you are learning about them and their philosophy towards breeding, they are also learning about you and determining whether they feel one of their kittens or cats would be a good match for you. The breeder will be interested in things such as whether you own your home or rent (they don't want one of their kids kicked out by an angry landlord with a no-pets clause!), whether you have children, your experience with cats in the past, your interests in showing or breeding, and your feelings about things like declawing or letting a cat roam outdoors. If you have had a pet before, the breeder may even ask to call your veterinarian for a reference. This introductory screening process is often done by phone, letter, fax, or e-mail. If the breeder feels comfortable, you will be invited to visit the cat or kitten that you are interested in.

Cat shows are excellent places to meet Tonkinese breeders and find the perfect cat for you.
Photo: Lorraine Shelton

When you visit the breeder, you may be greeted at the door by one or more of the feline family members. Photo: Isabelle Francais

VISITING THE BREEDER

When you visit the breeder, you will be looking at how sociable the cats in the household are and how healthy they appear to be. If the cattery is like most, you will be greeted at the door by one or more of the feline family members. Be alert—some Tonkinese have a habit of leaping onto the shoulders of the folks they take a liking to!

Keep in mind that the breeder is inviting you as a guest in her home. This is not a business to her—this is a member of her family that the two of you are discussing. Show the breeder the courtesy of being prompt and calling if you are not able to keep the appointment. The breeder will have determined, through her own experience with the cat or kittens, which one or ones she feels would be the best match for you, based on your preference for gender, color, and personality. The breeder's choice of which cat or kitten she feels would be best suited to your home is based on years of matching the right pet with someone just like you.

Do not be offended if the breeder does not give you a tour of the complete cattery. Respect the breeder's wishes to give mothers with young kittens and working stud males their privacy. The breeder also may not show you every cat or kitten she has available, although you should request to meet the parents of the kitten or cat you choose if they are on the premises.

WHAT AGE TO ADOPT A TONKINESE?

Most Tonkinese kittens will be ready for their new homes and available for adoption between 12 and 16 weeks of age. The breeder decides when each kitten is old enough for adoption based on his or her individual development. By the age of 12 weeks, the kitten has had her initial set of vaccinations,

The breeder may not give you a tour of the entire cattery, although you should request to meet the parents of your chosen kitten if they are on the premises. *Photo: Isabelle Francais*

has been taught to use the litter box by her mother, has a strong enough immune system to face the outside world, and is eating well on her own.

Bringing a kitten into your life is a delight that everyone should experience. But don't turn away from an older Tonkinese cat that may be available for adoption. If a cat that was promising in the show ring does not take well to the breeding life or does not produce kittens of exceptional quality, that cat may be offered for adoption. Breeders are often reluctant to part with these older friends, but they realize that while these cats must compete with others for lap time and playtime in their cattery, in a new home they can be the center of attention (and Tonkinese love to be the center of attention!) An adult Tonk may be the perfect cat for you.

Most Tonkinese kittens will be available for adoption between 12 and 16 weeks of age—about the same time that space in the kitty bed runs out! *Photo: Karen White*

THE GUIDE TO OWNING A TONKINESE CAT

You may wish to think about adopting an adult Tonkinese. With this playful breed, the fun doesn't stop after kittenhood. *Photo: Isabelle Francais*

Every Tonkinese deserves a playmate. If you aren't convinced that you can keep your new pet adequately entertained, consider adopting two wonderful Tonkinese. *Photo: Lorraine Shelton*

ONE TONK OR TWO?

If one Tonkinese is fun, a pair can be truly entertaining. If you tire of endless games of fetch and hide-and-seek, consider bringing in another Tonk to be a playmate for the first. If you aren't convinced that you can keep your Tonkinese adequately entertained, try adopting a pair instead of just one. Double the Tonks, double the fun! You'll be glad you took the plunge when you see your cats cuddled up in a sleepy pile or playing an energetic game of chase. The interaction between an older cat and a kitten can be especially delightful, as the grown-up cat teaches the younger one the joys of life while the younger cat brings out the "inner kitten" in the mature Tonkinese.

MALE OR FEMALE?

Tonkinese cats are wonderful pets in either gender, but you may find yourself drawn to one more than the other. Although personality traits overlap between the sexes, there are some generalizations that Tonk owners have developed. Some owners even feel that the different colors have different personalities. Male Tonkinese are especially devoted pets. They tend to be like little puppy dogs, following their owners around with great devotion, even in maturity. Females are often characterized as being more intelligent and cunning. They will frequently be the ringleaders in initiating mischief in the home. They are sweet and loving, though, and a female Tonkinese will enchant you with her feminine ways. As altered pets, the sexes get along fine with each other, although two females will sometimes exhibit a little tension.

WHAT "QUALITY" OF TONKINESE?

Every responsible breeder will give the same loving care, high-quality food, and conscientious health care to every kitten they breed, whether he or she is destined to be a show cat, a breeding cat, or a pet. Although all Tonk kittens are beautiful, not all fully represent the written standard by which the breed is judged at cat shows. Kittens that are not able to contribute to the advancement of the breed are called "pet quality" and are placed in homes as spayed or neutered pets. Most cat lovers who are new to the Tonkinese breed will have a hard time telling the pet-quality kittens apart from their show-quality littermates. Sometimes a cat will be placed as a pet because her color or pedigree does not fit in with a breeder's own program. Other kittens will be too much like a Siamese in type or too much like a Burmese in type to be shown. Others may have a minor cosmetic fault, such as a kink in the tail, that does not affect the health of the cat but should not be passed on to the next generation.

A show-quality Tonkinese will be of a color that may be shown in your association of choice and will be an excellent example of the breed. The breeder feels that this cat will be able to compete successfully against other Tonkinese and obtain the title of Champion or Grand Champion. The cat will have no disqualifying faults as listed in the Tonkinese standard.

"Breeding quality" is the term used for a cat that may not be successful at the shows, but that has superior characteristics that would make the cat valuable in a breeding program. Sometimes, the cat is simply the wrong color for competition but would have made a very successful show cat otherwise.

Sometimes a show-quality cat will be placed in a pet home specifically for the purpose of being shown in the altered or premiership cat classes in cat shows. A wonderful way to decide if you want to be a cat breeder yourself one day and to become more involved in the cat fancy is to show an altered cat in this type of competition. You will be able to demonstrate to other Tonkinese exhibitors that you are able to groom a Tonk well and keep your cat in top health and show condition. Tonkinese breeders may then be more willing to sell you a whole cat for showing and breeding and will be more likely to offer to mentor you in this rewarding hobby.

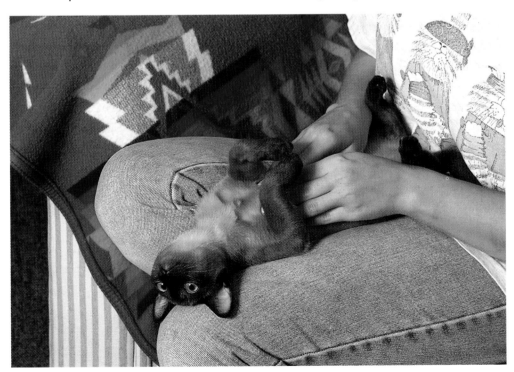

Whether male or female, the ideal Tonkinese cat will be a loving, intelligent pet. *Photo: Isabelle Francais*

SELECTING A TONKINESE CAT

General Care of Your Tonkinese

The proper care of a Tonkinese is similar to that of any cat. However, there are some special needs that Tonkinese have, and breeders that have worked with these cats for a long time have many suggestions that will help you keep your Tonkinese as healthy, beautiful, and happy as she can be. Although this book can serve as a general guide to taking care of your Tonkinese, you will want to consult with the breeder of your kitten for her advice on care as well. Following the breeder's suggestions on feeding, favorite playthings, grooming tips, and past litter box experience can make the transition to your home as pleasant as possible for your new pet.

Pet care professionals and owners understand that an indoor-only life is the most sensible, safest choice for cats. *Photo: Isabelle Francais*

In days past, cats were automatically allowed to roam outdoors. The perils of passing cars, other animals, and dangerous plants, among other threats, made the heartbreaking loss of a young pet a frequent experience. Nowadays, pet care professionals and owners understand that an indoor-only life for your cat is the most sensible choice. Your home can provide all the entertainment of the indoors, with the advantage of your close supervision, care, and protection.

ESSENTIAL SUPPLIES

There are some essential items that you will need before you bring a new cat into your home. Your Tonkinese will need to come home in a plastic carrier, so be sure to purchase one before you go to pick up your cat or kitten. This will be used in the future when you need to bring your cat to the vet, leave the house in the event of an emergency such as a fire, or otherwise transport her. Never travel with a cat loose in your car, because it is dangerous for both you and the cat.

Food and Water Dishes

You will need dishes for food and water. Ceramic, metal, or glass bowls are preferred to plastic, because they are easier to keep clean and do not collect the oils in the food. The use of plastic feeding dishes has been linked to chin acne in cats.

Litter Box

When choosing a litter box, consider the size of your new Tonkinese. A young kitten should not be faced with having to climb the imposing sides of the largest size of litter box.

Your Tonkinese will need to come home in a plastic carrier. Purchase one before you go to pick up your cat or kitten. *Photo: Isabelle Francais*

Purchase a small box first. As your kitten grows, she can then be introduced to a larger litter box.

Litter

There are dozens of different types of litter available. It is a good idea to use the same brand of litter that the cat is already accustomed to using when you first bring your Tonkinese home. Scoopable clay litters should not be used with kittens under four months of age. Heavily scented litters may be unattractive to your cat and may lead to improper elimination habits.

Litter Box Maintenance

The key to making sure your cat continues to use her litter box is to keep it clean. Cats are fastidious animals. Scoop out solid wastes every day and replace the litter

Plastic feeding dishes like these are not recommended. They have been linked to chin acne in cats.

completely when it becomes no more than one-third soiled with urine. If a cat does not have a clean litter box, she may choose to do her business on the nice clean living room carpet! Disinfecting the litter box when the litter is changed is an excellent idea for both the health of your cat and to eliminate odors. After washing the litter box completely with soap and water, spray it with a solution of one part bleach to ten parts water. Let it sit for 15 minutes and then rinse well. Never use a disinfectant containing phenols on any surface that your cat will be exposed to, because these are very toxic to your cat. These include pine oil-based cleaners. Do not add bleach directly to a dirty litter box, because the bleach will combine with the ammonia in the urine to form toxic chlorine gas. Clean the litter box first before adding bleach to it.

Make sure your cat can easily find and access the litter box. When you first bring your new Tonkinese home, you may wish to keep her confined to a portion of your home, close to her food, water, and litter box. Once she learns where these items are, she can be allowed access to a larger area. Remember, just like young humans, kittens must use the litter box frequently, and they cannot be expected to "hold it" until they climb upstairs or across a large house. One litter box per cat and at least one litter box for every floor of a house is a good general rule.

Scratching Posts

Your Tonkinese will enjoy a scratching post, and this essential item will also help save your furniture from harm. You will want to make sure that the post is the most attractive item in the house to the cat and something with which she will want to exercise this instinctual behavior. The post should be a minimum of four feet high so that your Tonkinese can reach up high to scratch at it. The best posts have a variety of scratching surfaces, including rough sisal rope, heavy carpet, and perhaps even natural tree trunks. A soft, fluffy scratching post may be the most attractive to you, but rough, hard surfaces are usually more attractive to your cat.

A small, plain litter box like this one will be adequate for most cats. Of course, there are plenty of other types available if you want a fancier box for your beloved pet.

The best scratching posts are made of a variety of scratching surfaces, including rough sisal rope, heavy carpet, and even natural tree trunks. *Photo: Isabelle Francais*

Tonkinese cats love toys! A game of "kitty fishing" can give your cat exercise and help to develop a bond between you and your pet.
Photo: Isabelle Francais

Experiment to find which types of surface your cat prefers. If she is still using your best couch, you haven't found the right post yet!

Harness and Leash

You may want to purchase a harness and a leash for your Tonkinese. These cats tend to take to walking on a leash more willingly than many other breeds. Make sure the harness fits well and securely. Let your cat get used to wearing the harness first, and then let her drag the leash around the house under your close supervision, so that it does not catch on anything. Practice your walks in the house before trying this outside. Accompanying you on a leash is a safe way for your cat to explore the great outdoors without the risks to life and limb that free-roaming cats face every day.

All cats can get into mischief, and Tonkinese cats are no exception. Keep your cat from harm by minimizing the hazards present in your home. *Photo: Isabelle Francais*

Toys

Of course, we can't forget about toys! Not only are toys entertaining for your cat, they can also help develop a bond between you and your Tonkinese. An energetic game of "kitty fishing," where a feather or other toy is attached to the end of a piece of string dangling from a pole, can also help develop and maintain muscle tone in your Tonkinese. You'll be surprised at how easy it will be to get your Tonk airborne! This breed is also known for its excellent fetching ability, so make sure you get plenty of small furry toys for this activity. Anything that rolls, wiggles, or bounces is bound to get the attention of your Tonkinese. The games you can play with your cat are limited only by your imagination.

CAT-PROOFING YOUR HOME

Cats can get into mischief, and we must be sure to keep them from harm by minimizing the hazards present in any home. Plastic covers for electric outlets are easy to find and are worth the few cents they cost. Make sure that you do not bring any toxic plants into your home, because Tonkinese cats love to chew on houseplants. Common toxic plants include: amaryllis, azalea, calla lily, daffodil, English ivy, foxglove, holly, honeysuckle, hyacinth, iris, morning glory, mistletoe, periwinkle, philodendron, poinsettia, rhododendron, oleander, tobacco, and wisteria.

Your cat may perceive fragile items placed on high shelves as a challenge—she just might get great enjoyment out of breaking them. Fireplaces must have screens, because they can be dangerous to a cat that is trying to get

Your cat may perceive fragile items on high shelves as a challenge. Make sure to keep valuables out of her reach. *Photo: Isabelle Francais*

warm. This will also protect your carpet from a kitten playing in the ashes. Keep your sewing items in a separate room, away from where your cat lives. Tonks love to play with string, yarn, ribbon, and thread, but these items, when ingested, can cause great damage to the cat's intestines, especially if there are needles attached. Tinsel from a Christmas tree can be deadly, because its sharp edges can cause life-threatening cuts in the intestinal tract. Many cleaning products can be harmful if ingested by a cat, so be sure to keep them where your cat cannot get to them. Because Tonkinese are notorious for learning how to open cabinet doors and kitchen drawers, you may want to put the same kind of latches on them that are used by parents with young children.

Feeding and Nutrition

When you take your new Tonkinese home, you will want to provide her with the same diet that she was eating before she came to you. If you decide to change to another brand or type of food, do so slowly by mixing in the new diet with the old for a few days. Your Tonkinese will look and feel her best if you provide her with a premium brand of cat food. In order to maintain the good muscle tone that is characteristic of this breed, your cat will need a food that contains high-quality protein from easily digestible sources. Be sure that you purchase cat food that obtains its protein from meat sources, such as chicken or lamb, rather than from vegetable sources such as soy protein. Cats are carnivores and need the essential nutrients provided by meat. Tonkinese cats can have sensitive stomachs, so be on the alert for signs, such as vomiting and diarrhea, that a particular food is not agreeing well with your cat. Fish-based foods can be a common culprit when a cat has an upset stomach.

Although your cat's main diet should consist of a commercial cat food that is scientifically designed to meet all of your cat's nutritional needs, a very small amount of supplementation with table foods can be enjoyable for both you and your cat. These should be considered treats and not given in large quantities. Cooked meats are particularly popular, of course, but you may find that your cat also enjoys a small nibble of cantaloupe, bread, pasta, or a particular vegetable. Cats are not capable of properly digesting cow's milk, and feeding it to them can result in diarrhea. A small amount of goat's milk, however, can be given as a special treat and is tolerated by a cat's digestive system.

Your Tonkinese will do well on either dry or canned cat food. Dry food can help keep your cat's teeth in good condition, so it is usually recommended as the main staple of your cat's diet. Many owners put out a bowl of dry kibble that is available to the cat at all times, with canned food as an optional

Your cat's main diet should consist of a commercial cat food that is scientifically designed to meet her nutritional needs. *Photo: Isabelle Francais*

supplement. This works particularly well for a growing kitten, but you may need to control the amount of food an adult cat gets if she starts to put on too much weight. If you feed your cat canned food, be sure to remove any remaining portion after the cat has finished her meal to prevent the cat from eating spoiled food.

You may also give your cat meals at specific times during the day. A young kitten will need as many as four or five meals a day, while an adult cat may do best on two meals a day. Fresh, clear water should be available to your cat at all times. Food and water should be kept far away from the litter box, because cats do not like to eliminate and eat in the same area.

With a premium commercial food as your cat's main diet, vitamin supplements will be unnecessary. In fact, you can upset the balance of the nutrients in the food with incorrect supplementation. Discuss any vitamin or mineral supplements with your veterinarian before using them.

Young kittens, nursing mothers, and pregnant queens should be fed a diet specifically made to fulfill their nutritional needs, one that is usually labeled "for kittens" or "for growth." Such a diet should state on the label: "Animal feeding tests substantiate that this diet provides complete and balanced nutrition for all life stages." There are also diets designed to help control the weight of an overweight cat as well as diets specifically designed for elderly cats. A veterinary prescription diet may be recommended by your vet to help with a chronic health problem.

It was once believed that male cats should be fed canned food exclusively to prevent them from developing urinary problems. Luckily, commercial cat foods are now formulated to make these problems no more common with feeding dry food than with feeding canned food. Soft-moist foods can be used as an occasional treat but should not be a cat's primary diet. These foods have been linked to a particular form of anemia in kittens and elderly cats. A cat that is sick and refusing to eat may accept meat baby foods as a temporary diet. Avoid brands that contain onion powder, because this ingredient causes health problems in cats.

Many owners feed their cats small daily amounts of canned food in addition to leaving dry food out at all times. *Photo: Isabelle Francais*

THE GUIDE TO OWNING A TONKINESE CAT

A kitten will need as many as four or five meals a day, while an adult cat may do best on two meals a day.
Photo: Isabelle Francais

Kittens, nursing mothers, and pregnant queens require special diets to meet their increased need for calories and nutrients. *Photo: Karen White*

Grooming Your Tonkinese

Tonkinese are one of the easiest breeds of cat to groom. Exhibitors call them "wash and wear" cats because it doesn't take much effort to get them looking beautiful for cat shows. It is a good idea to get your cat used to the essential elements of grooming while she is young. This will make it much easier to keep her looking beautiful throughout her lifetime.

NAILS

It is important to keep your Tonkinese cat's nails trimmed. This will save wear and tear on your furniture as well as keep her more

Tonkinese cats are one of the easiest breeds to groom—they do most of the work themselves!
Photo: Isabelle Francais

THE GUIDE TO OWNING A TONKINESE CAT

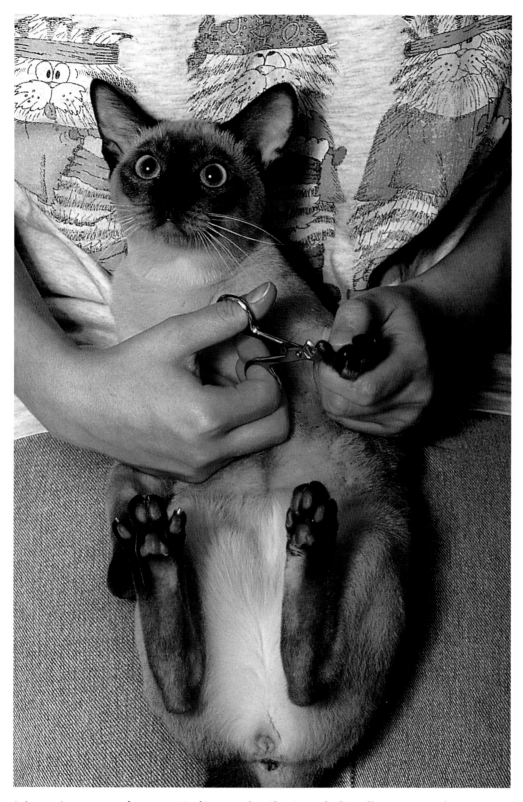

It is very important to keep your Tonkinese cat's nails trimmed. This will save wear and tear on your **furniture.** *Photo: Isabelle Francais*

Most cats enjoy being groomed with a rubber brush or comb, and this provides quality time for both pet and owner. *Photo: Isabelle Francais*

comfortable. It is recommended that the nails be clipped on a weekly basis. Extend each nail one at a time by squeezing the end of the paw. Look carefully at the nail, and you will see a pink vein running through two-thirds of it. With a pair of nail trimmers designed for the purpose or a pair of nail trimmers designed for human nails, clip off the tip of each nail, just past where the blood vessel ends. If you accidentally cut into the vein, don't panic. Styptic powder, which is designed to stop this type of bleeding, is sold right next to the nail trimmers. It is a good idea to keep some of this powder on hand for emergencies. In a pinch, a dab of flour will serve the purpose almost as well.

If you are uncomfortable tackling this procedure for the first time, ask the breeder of your kitten, a pet groomer, or your veterinarian to demonstrate it for you.

Surgical declawing, a mutilation of the cat's feet that involves the removal of the most distal bone and joint of each toe, should not be considered in an active cat like the Tonkinese. Most breeders' contracts will stipulate that their cats must not be declawed, and declawing is actually illegal in most countries outside of the United States.

BATHING

Trimming your cat's nails before bath time is an excellent way to make sure that you don't accidentally get scratched during the bath.

An occasional bath will keep your Tonkinese looking her best and is a must when going to a show. There are many excellent cat shampoos on the market, and a brand with conditioners will make your cat especially silky. Some cats, especially

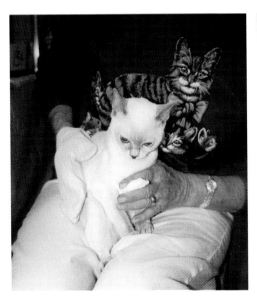

A chamois glove gives this platinum mink Tonkinese a special glow before that all-important trip to the show ring. *Photo: Lorraine Shelton*

intact males, will benefit from a degreasing shampoo before the conditioning shampoo. Experimenting with different shampoos will allow you to find the best one for your cat.

BRUSHING AND GROOMING

Grooming your Tonkinese can be an enjoyable component of the quality time you spend with your cat. Your cat loves to be petted, of course, and most Tonkinese enjoy the feel of the rubber brush that becomes an extension of your loving hands. A rubber brush will remove old, dead hair and stimulate the growth of new, shiny hair. A final rub with a chamois cloth to smooth the coat down in the direction that it grows is an exhibitor's secret to giving your cat that final special glow. Chamois cloths can be found in the car care department, or try the gloves made of chamois that are carried by stores that cater to the serious cat exhibitor.

Grooming time provides a good opportunity to check on your cat's health as well. Feel her weight and muscle tone and check for any abnormal lumps, bumps, or skin changes. A quick swab of the ear with a cotton ball or swab will keep them clean and make you aware of any black discharge that could be the sign of ear mites. Check the nose to make sure that no discharge has collected, which is a possible sign of a respiratory infection. Check the eyes for clarity and lack of discharge or redness.

DENTAL CARE

Pet owners, with the help of their veterinarians, are beginning to understand the importance of taking care of their cat's teeth. Regular brushing with a special toothbrush and paste designed for pets can help reduce the number of professional teeth cleaning visits to the veterinarian. This is another important part of grooming and health care that is best introduced when the cat is young. Check regularly for signs of inflamed gums or tartar buildup.

During grooming sessions, check your cat's ears for signs of ear mites. *Photo: Isabelle Francais*

Health Care

The Tonkinese is a very healthy and vigorous breed of cat. However, like any living thing, your cat can become ill. Breeders do their very best to raise healthy kittens, but viruses and other infections can lurk invisibly in any situation where multiple animals are

Stress, viruses, parasites, and household dangers can all make your Tonkinese kitten or cat sick. Good preventive care will avoid many common feline maladies. *Photo: Isabelle Francais*

kept. Some viruses linger in the cat's body for long periods of time and do not normally make your Tonkinese sick, but these can blossom under stressful conditions. Pests, such as fleas or mosquitoes entering your house from the outside world, can harm your cat. Your own home can harbor potential hazards, such as poisonous plants or toxic cleaning chemicals. There are many precautions that you can take to keep your Tonkinese healthy and to make sure that minor ailments do not become more severe. Your cat can be protected against viral diseases with vaccinations and saved from parasitic infestation through preventive care. Appropriate attention to other potential dangers can prevent many situations that can threaten your cat's health. With proper care, an indoor-only environment, and good medical attention, you should be able to look forward to 10, 15, and even close to 20 years of companionship with your Tonkinese.

For minor cuts and scratches caused by roughhousing, an antibiotic ointment may come in handy.
Photo: Isabelle Francais

FIRST AID

There are some items that you will need to have on hand in case of a feline emergency. A thermometer that is just for cat use will come in handy for determining if your cat is running a fever. Have an assistant gently restrain the cat by the nape of the neck. Lubricate the end of the thermometer with petroleum jelly and gently place it approximately half an inch into the cat's rectum. Wait a couple of minutes, remove it, and note the temperature. The newer electronic thermometers are especially easy to use and worth the investment. A cat's normal body temperature is 99.5 to 101.5° F (37.5 to 38.6° C). If the reading is outside of this range, contact your veterinarian immediately. A fever or depressed temperature can be life-threatening and is the sign of a serious health problem.

Tonkinese can roughhouse very seriously with each other, and the occasional small cut or scratch is not unusual. For minor injuries, an antibiotic ointment will come in handy. Other items that can keep your cat's injuries or ailments controlled until a veterinarian can be consulted include gauze and adhesive tape to control bleeding, styptic powder to control bleeding if a nail is cut too closely during grooming, sterile saline solution to rinse out the eyes if something gets in them, and tweezers.

IS YOUR CAT SICK?

Tonkinese cats are very healthy as a rule. However, you will want to keep an observant eye out for any signs that your cat is not feeling well. Signs that your cat needs a trip to the vet include:

• Lethargy
• Discharge from the eyes or nose

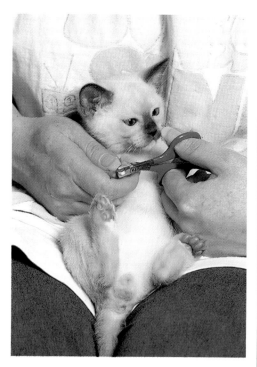

Styptic powder is a useful product to keep around in case you clip your cat's claw too closely.
Photo: Isabelle Francais

- Third eyelid protraction
- Persistent scratching or biting at a part of the body
- A body part that feels hot
- Limping
- Swelling
- Vomiting
- Abnormal stools
- More than occasional sneezing, or the sneezing of thick or colored mucus
- Bleeding
- Unusual vocalization

DISEASES OF THE CAT AND VACCINATION

Vaccinations are your cat's best defense against many diseases that can threaten her health. Your kitten will come from her breeder having received her first set of shots. Your cat's breeder will give you the dates your kitten or cat was vaccinated so that you may give this information to your vet. Although vaccine schedules can vary, most kittens will need to receive inoculations at 9, 12, and 16 weeks of age. A booster vaccination will be needed a year later.

The essential set of vaccinations that your cat will receive includes protection against panleukopenia, calicivirus, and rhinotracheitis. These are usually combined in a single shot. Thereafter, your pet cat will need to receive vaccinations once every three years. New research on vaccine effectiveness has shown that cats do not

Examine your Tonkinese regularly from the time that she is a kitten to check for signs that she is ill.
Photo: Isabelle Francais

need vaccinations every year. Despite this, your cat will still need a complete health exam by your veterinarian at least once a year, and more frequently for older cats. Your vet is qualified to notice health problems at their beginning stages, before they become serious.

Panleukopenia
Commonly called "cat distemper" or "cat flu," panleukopenia has been virtually eliminated through the use of modern vaccines. This disease is caused by a parvovirus. Unfortunately, because this disease has become so rare, some have questioned the necessity of vaccinating their cats at all. This attitude led to an outbreak of panleukopenia in California in the late 1990s among Tonkinese catteries that had become lax in vaccinating against the disease. The vaccine is the most effective of all cat vaccines, with the lowest rate of adverse reactions. Like most feline vaccines, the panleukopenia vaccine comes in both a killed form and a modified live form. The modified live form of this vaccine should not be used where there are pregnant queens, with immunocompromised or sick cats, or when killed vaccine is being used on other cats in the home at the same time.

Calicivirus and Herpesvirus (Rhinotracheitis)
The two viruses most commonly responsible for respiratory infections in cats are calicivirus and a herpesvirus commonly called rhinotracheitis. They can both cause sneezing and nasal discharge. However, calicivirus infection can also cause limping, while rhinotracheitis can attack the eyes, causing conjunctivitis and corneal ulcers. Vaccination will greatly reduce the severity of symptoms but often does not completely prevent the disease. Killed vaccines cause fewer side effects than modified live vaccines but appear to be less effective. The most effective type of vaccine is one given directly into the nasal passages. This type of vaccine may cause minor symptoms a few days later (sneezing, for example) but is extremely effective in preventing the disease in the future. Despite the fact that rhinotracheitis is caused by a herpesvirus, this disease is unrelated to the disease of the same name in people.

Chlamydia
Another infectious agent that can cause

Unusual vocalization is just one sign of possible illness or injury in your cat. *Photo: Isabelle Francais*

respiratory symptoms in cats is chlamydia. The most common symptom is conjunctivitis. This is not considered a true virus but is unlike a bacteria because it must be inside of a cell to survive. Until recently, medications used to treat chlamydia (erythromycin, enrofloxacin, and the tetracyclines) had to be given for a long period of time and were not always effective. Newer drugs, such as azithromycin, are extremely effective against chlamydial infection. Although vaccines against chlamydia are available, their efficacy is poor and their rate of side effects is high.

Bordatella

Bordatella is a recently discovered cause of serious respiratory infections in cats and is caused by a bacteria. Previously considered to be only a dog disease, it

Both viral and chlamydial infections can cause conjunctivitis, which is evidenced by sore, swollen eyes and a thick discharge. *Photo: Isabelle Francais*

appears that bordatella is not uncommon in cats. An effective vaccine against this disease is now available and may be recommended by your vet. The vaccine should be strongly considered if you will be showing your cat, because this disease appears to be spread at cat shows. Azithromycin also appears to be the drug of choice in treating bordatella in cats.

Rabies

Rabies is one of the very few diseases that is transmissible from cats to humans. In some areas, vaccination against rabies is required by law. If your cat will be traveling by plane or across state or country borders, you will also need to vaccinate against rabies. To avoid exposure to rabies, your cat should be kept inside, except when under supervision. Rabies is endemic in some areas, and your vet can advise you if the wildlife in your area may be affected. Because the rabies vaccine is associated with a rare form of cancer, it should only be given when it is needed.

Feline Infectious Peritonitis

Feline infectious peritonitis (FIP) is a heartbreaking and fatal disease of cats. Kittens and young cats within their first two years of life are the most susceptible to this virus, and cats from large catteries or shelter situations are especially at risk. Unfortunately, although a vaccine is available for this disease, it appears to be ineffective in most instances, because kittens are usually infected with the causative agent of the disease before the

Responsible breeders help minimize the incidence of diseases like FIP by keeping small numbers of cats in immaculate conditions. *Photo: Isabelle Francais*

age at which a vaccine is effective. Cats do not catch the actual FIP virus from another cat. Instead, they catch a benign virus called a coronavirus, often from their mothers. It is unknown why the vast majority of cats can tolerate infection with this virus, while in a rare few the virus turns into the lethal disease FIP. Once a cat begins to exhibit symptoms of this disease, it inevitably proceeds on to death, although the quality and length of life can be improved with medication.

Breeders can help minimize the incidence of this disease in their kittens by keeping as small a cattery as possible, keeping cats in small, isolated groups within the cattery, breeding from only the healthiest of cats, avoiding inbreeding, and isolating each mother with her kittens from other cats in the home. There is no reliable test available to enable a cattery to eliminate this disease from their population of cats or to determine if a healthy cat is at risk for dying of FIP. Any test that purports to serve this purpose should be regarded with skepticism.

Feline Leukemia

This viral disease is fatal to cats, although cats may remain without symptoms for many years after infection. Unlike FIP, for which a reliable test is not available, breeders have been able to eliminate this disease from their catteries by testing all incoming cats to ensure that they are free from this virus. A test for feline leukemia (FeLV) should be a part of the initial health exam by your veterinarian when you first

Feline leukemia is spread through a cat's repetitive, intimate contact with a carrier cat. It is not spread through screen doors, at cat shows, or by bringing it indoors on your shoes. *Photo: Isabelle Francais*

bring your cat home. For the most accurate results, ask that this test be performed on your cat's serum (the liquid part of blood), rather than on whole blood, tears, or saliva. If you have other cats in your household, your new cat should be isolated (or, preferably, not brought home) until the test is performed. A vaccine is available against feline leukemia. This disease is spread through a cat's repetitive, intimate contact with a carrier cat. It is not spread through screen doors, at cat shows, or by bringing it indoors on your shoes. Catteries have worked very hard to eliminate this disease from the cat fancy. Because your cat is a product of this rigorous testing program and will not go outdoors to interact with untested cats, the feline leukemia vaccine may not be recommended for your cat. This vaccine is needed in cats that roam outdoors or where untested cats are brought into the home. Because the feline leukemia vaccine, like the rabies vaccine, is associated with a rare form of cancer, it should only be given when indicated.

Fleas

Flea control has become much less of a challenge with the new products that have recently come on the market. Traditionally, pyrethrin-containing flea sprays, shampoos, dips, bombs, and carpet sprays were part of a yearly ritual that began with the first warm days of spring and continued until the coldest part of winter struck. These approaches are still valuable for the immediate removal of fleas from your cat and your home, but for the prevention of reinfestation, a monthly pill, or drops applied to the back of your cat's neck, can be more convenient, less stressful to your cat, more effective, and less toxic than the old methods. Some of these preparations can even protect your cat against ear mites or internal parasites as well. Discuss with your veterinarian which flea control approach would be best for your cat and appropriate for the parasite challenges in your area. Never apply a product labeled "for dogs only" on your cat. Some of these products, although safe for dogs, may be lethal to cats.

Intestinal Parasites

Intestinal parasites are occasionally seen in cats. *Tapeworms* are carried by fleas, so conscientious flea protection will also protect your cat against tapeworms. If you have had an outbreak of fleas in your home, your veterinarian may recommend that your cat be treated for tapeworms, usually with a drug called Droncit (pyrantel palmoate). You may see signs of this parasite—segmented worms in your cat's stool, or segments that look like grains of rice around your cat's anus.

The other common intestinal parasite seen in cats is the *roundworm*. This is diagnosed by examining a sample of your cat's feces under a microscope. Your vet may ask you to bring in a small stool sample from your cat's litter box when you bring

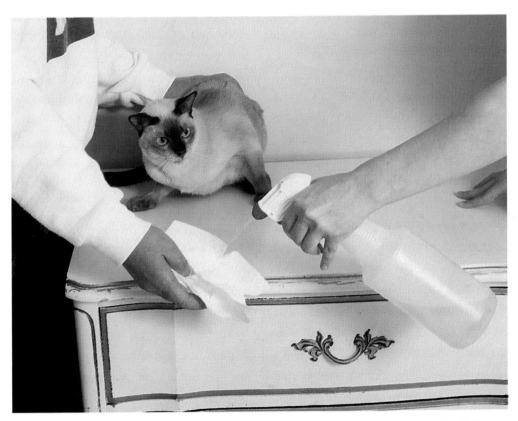

It's no longer necessary to use messy flea sprays, shampoos, dips, bombs, and so forth with all the new flea prevention products that have recently come on the market. *Photo: Isabelle Francais*

her for her annual checkup. You should also bring a stool sample to your vet if worms are seen in your cat's stool or if your cat is showing signs of intestinal problems.

In areas where there are mosquitoes, you will want to protect your cat against *heartworm*, a parasite spread through mosquito bites. Given monthly, a liquid oral dose, pill, or solution applied to the back of the cat's neck will protect your cat against this deadly disease. Ask your veterinarian if your cat may be at risk.

Ringworm

Not caused by a parasite at all but by a fungus, ringworm infection can occasionally be found in cats obtained from any multi-cat situation. It is most commonly seen in young kittens. Care must be taken in handling affected cats, because this fungus can cause skin lesions on people as well. The disease is self-limiting, meaning that it will clear up on its own as the cat's immune system learns to combat the infection. However, in order to limit the spread of this disease, an infected cat should be treated both topically and systemically. Effective topical treatments include dips comprised of lime-sulfur, antifungal ointments, or antifungal shampoos. Although sulfur dips are smelly and messy, they have been shown to be the most effective topical treatment of ringworm. Systemic treatment of ringworm is accomplished by administering an antifungal drug to your cat orally. The safest drugs to combat ringworm are the newer azole drugs, such as fluconazole or itraconazole. These work more quickly and are more effective than the griseofulvin or ketoconazole drugs used in the past.

Giardia and Coccidia

Diarrhea in your cat can have many causes, and one of these one-celled parasites may be one of them. Infection occurs when a cat ingests cysts or eggs in food, water, feces, or soil. Diarrhea may be chronic or intermittent and may contain mucus or blood. Other symptoms include weight loss, listlessness, intestinal gas, or loss of appetite. Some animals may carry these parasites and show no clinical signs. A diagnosis is made by examining a fresh (less than 2 hours old) fecal sample under the microscope. These infections have proven to be frustrating to both pet owners and veterinarians because of drug resistance and the strong likelihood of reinfection. Giardia cysts are very resistant to destruction and remain in the environment year'round. Oral drugs such as metronidazole, fenbendazole, or sulfadimethoxine can be used to treat this disease.

Toxoplasmosis

One parasite that has gotten a lot of publicity is the organism with the scientific name of *Toxoplasma gondii*. If a pregnant woman becomes exposed to this parasite during her pregnancy, there is a rare chance that the infection will cause birth defects in her unborn child. While a woman is pregnant, she can avoid exposure by wearing gloves while cleaning the litter box, washing hands after contact with cat feces, or (the most popular option) delegating litter box duties to another family member during the course of the pregnancy.

Luckily, toxoplasmosis infection does not occur in strictly indoor cats that are fed a commercial diet. It can occur in cats that hunt outdoors or that are fed a raw meat diet. After becoming infected with the parasite, a cat may shed infectious eggs in her feces for up to two weeks. After that time, the cat is immune to infection and can no longer pass this disease to humans.

Hairballs

A common cause of vomiting in cats is the buildup of hair in the stomach. This happens when the cat grooms herself. Frequent brushing with a rubber brush to remove dead hair from your Tonkinese's coat will minimize this accumulation of fur. If hairballs become a problem, they can be treated with a hairball remedy paste, given to your cat on an empty stomach. These pastes are formulated to be very palatable to cats, so administration is usually not at all difficult. Most cats will voluntarily lick a ribbon of this paste from your finger. If not, the paste can be put on the cat's upper lip or paw, where she will lick it off.

SPAYING AND NEUTERING

With current veterinary anesthetics and proper technique, your kitten may be altered anytime after the age of eight weeks. In fact, recovery from this procedure is much faster in young kittens than when surgery is done at the age of six months to a year. Altering should take place before your kitten reaches sexual maturity. Tonkinese can be early to mature, so it is a good idea to alter your kitten between two and six months of age. This is the only way to avoid the health consequences of a female coming into heat and the behavioral consequences of a male developing the bad habit of spraying urine around the house to mark his territory. A female kitten that has been allowed to come into heat is at risk for breast cancer later in life. Once a male cat has started to spray, this can be a very difficult habit to break. Early altering can help ensure that your cat has the healthiest, happiest life possible.

It's a myth that spaying and neutering will make your cat fat and lazy. Adequate exercise and a good diet will prevent obesity.
Photo: Isabelle Francais

Breeding and Showing Tonkinese Cats

Living with a Tonkinese is a special joy. Sharing your love of the breed with other pedigreed cat fanciers is a fulfilling hobby that will help you take your cat-oriented activities to a new level.

You may have every confidence that your Tonkinese is the most beautiful cat in the world, but there is a memorable delight in seeing a professional cat judge share your appreciation of the beauty of your cat.

Sharing your love of the Tonkinese breed with other pedigreed cat fanciers is a fulfilling hobby that you may wish to pursue. *Photo: Lorraine Shelton*

The decision to breed your cat should not be made lightly. Responsible breeders have a passionate wish to make a positive contribution to the breed. *Photo: Karen White*

Breeding cats is not a moneymaking venture. With all the costs involved in raising a litter of kittens and finding homes for them, very few breeders manage to break even. *Photo: Lorraine Shelton*

Whether you come home with an armload of ribbons or just a greater appreciation of your pet, exhibiting at cat shows can be a very rewarding experience.

Another aspect of the cat fancy in which you may wish to participate is breeding. Joining in the community of cat breeders can bring a whole new spectrum of emotions to your life, from the thrilling birth of the next generation of the Tonkinese breed to heartbreaking sorrow at the cruelties Mother Nature can bring to the birthing process. The decision to breed your cat should not be made lightly, because the healthiest and happiest life for your cat is as a spayed or neutered pet. However, many people find the propagation and improvement of the Tonkinese through selective, responsible breeding to be very rewarding. After choosing the most appropriate mate for their pet, their decisions are reflected in new life that joins the world nine short weeks later.

BREEDING

The most important part of breeding is developing a relationship with an experienced breeder who will become your mentor. If you are considering breeding, you will begin with a female of breeding or show quality, because a male will not be happy without a steady stream of females to keep him company. A male is, therefore, not appropriate to start with. Your mentor can provide a male to breed to your female when the time comes. This is called "stud service" in the cat fancy. Do not enter into breeding without giving the matter a great deal of thought. Your cycling female will be very noisy and may spray urine in the house before she is old enough to breed. A

Cat breeders attend cat shows to receive feedback from the judges on the progress of their breeding program. *Photo: Lorraine Shelton*

Is the world of cat shows perfect for you and your Tonkinese? Many cat lovers thrive in the circus atmosphere of a big international show like this one. *Photo: Isabelle Francais*

It all starts with one rosette. Here, GC, RW Vanwin Forevr Krystal of Karessence poses with her very first award. *Photo: Karen White*

breeding cat has health challenges that a neutered pet will never have. A breeder must be able to deal with both new life and death and have the time and resources to attend to the queen and her kittens and find the little ones good homes.

Breeding cats is not a moneymaking venture and is actually a very expensive hobby. By the time you add up the costs of stud service, veterinary care, additional food and litter, and advertising the kittens for sale, very few breeders can break even on a litter, let alone make money. A cesarean section in the middle of the night is a very real possibility. This can cost hundreds of dollars, with no guarantees of live kittens or even a live queen afterward.

Breeders pursue this hobby because of a love for the breed. In their minds, they have a picture of the perfect cat. They breed their cats for the purpose of creating that cat. Just as an artist uses a palate of colors to create a painting, cat breeders use a palate of cat genes to create living works of art. A responsible breeder attends cat shows in order to receive qualified opinions on their progress from other breeders and judges and to determine the next step in their breeding program.

SHOWING

Do you think that your Tonkinese just might be the prettiest one in town? Do you plan on breeding Tonkinese one day? Are you anxious to meet other Tonkinese owners (and their cats) and learn more about the Tonkinese standard? If so, you may want to participate in the fun and exciting sport of exhibiting your cat at cat shows, where cat lovers just like you get together to share their passion for felines.

Shows are held by cat clubs associated with a particular cat registry. The four largest ones in the United States and Canada are the Cat Fanciers' Association (CFA), The International Cat Association (TICA), the Canadian Cat Association (CCA), and the American Cat Fanciers Association (ACFA). In Europe, clubs may be members of Federation Internationale Feline (FIFe), the Governing Council of the Cat Fancy (GCCF), or the World Cat Federation (WCF). The most successful cats at shows held in each association over the course of the show year (which runs from May to April in the US) are commonly recognized with coveted awards and additional titles to add their names, such as National Winner, Regional Winner, or International Winner. Each year, the very best kittens, championship cats, and premiership (altered) cats are honored with these awards at a banquet held in their honor.

Along the way to these ultimate awards, cats compete for titles that may take from one to many shows to attain. Depending on the association, the titles include Champion (usually attained by defeating other cats of your breed), Grand Champion (which requires defeating top cats of other breeds), and Supreme Grand Champion (which requires a declaration of Best Cat in Show by a judge). Altered cats also compete for equivalent titles among themselves: Premier, Grand Premier, or Grand Champion Alter, for example.

If you think you may be interested in showing, be sure the breeder of your cat is aware of this and can provide you with a cat with no disqualifying features that is an excellent example of the breed. Your cat cannot have a kinked tail, and whole males must have both testicles descended, for example. Showing a neutered male is an especially good way to start in this hobby, as these are more commonly available for purchase than whole cats.

Finding a Cat Show
To obtain the date and location of a cat show near you, refer to one of the various monthly cat magazines that are available, or contact the cat associations directly. The cat associations also have Web sites where their show schedules are listed. Each cat show listing, whether in print or on the Web, will have a contact phone number. That person, usually the entry clerk, can supply you with an entry form, answer your questions, and help you enter the show. Entry forms may also be downloaded from the Internet or obtained from the cat associations. The listing will also name the judges who are officiating at the show and state the location of the show. Make sure you obtain a copy of the show rules from the association in which you will show. This will list the class number that you will use

If you are interested in showing, acquire a show-quality cat from your breeder rather than a pet-quality cat. *Photo: Isabelle Francais*

A comfortable cage environment will help keep your cat relaxed while she is at the show.
Photo: Karen White

on the entry form, identifying the color and gender of your cat, among other important things you will need to know. You must state on the entry form whether your cat is a kitten (starting at three or four months of age and concluding at eight or nine months of age, depending on the association), a championship cat (whole cats that are over the age limit for kittens), or a premiership/alter cat (spayed or neutered cats that are over the age limit for kittens).

Types of Cat Shows

Not all cat shows are formatted the same way. Some are one-day shows, and others are held over two or three days. Some shows are limited to one breed of cat, but most are open to all breeds. Within a show, one or many judges may handle a cat over the course of the weekend. These details, a description of the awards given, and rules unique to a particular show will be listed in the show flyer, which is distributed at other shows or mailed to past cat show participants. When you contact the entry clerk about the show, he or she will mail you a show flyer. Show flyers are also often placed on the Internet.

Pre-Show Preparations

Your cat's breeder will be your most valuable resource in getting your cat ready for the show. She will be able to give you advice on grooming, cat show etiquette, and supplies that you will need to bring. Among these are a carrier in which to transport your cat; a small bottle of disinfectant; paper towels; material to cover the top, bottom, and sides of the cage you will be provided with; cat food; a cat bed or blanket; a small litter tray; food and water dishes; grooming equipment; cat toys; and pens. Don't forget brushes, combs, chamois cloth, facial tissues, and other grooming supplies. Litter will be provided at the show. If you forget something, don't panic. Almost every show features at least one vendor selling all kinds of show supplies at very reasonable prices.

It is a good idea to attend a show or two before you enter one. Find the Tonkinese breeders and introduce yourself. Tonk folks are known for being particularly friendly, just like their cats. Bring pictures of your cats to get the opinion of other breeders on your cat's potential to succeed in the show ring. If they gently advise you that your cat is not up to show standards, it does not make your cat any less of a wonderful pet. The show ring is extremely competitive, and the subtleties that make a top show cat differ from a more ordinary cat are not easy for a novice to recognize. By continuing to attend shows, you can make your acquaintance with those who can help you obtain a cat closer to the written standard. It will also help you to develop a trained eye to be able to recognize a cat with show potential yourself.

Once you are entered in the show and have all your supplies gathered, you must make sure that your cat is ready. She will have been bathed, groomed, and her claws will have been clipped. The clipping of claws is an important show rule to protect judges from harm if a cat becomes frightened. Some cats look their best if they are bathed the day before the show, while others look better when bathed a few days before the show. Try a "dress rehearsal" before the show to find out which is best for your cat. The other important way in which your cat is prepared for the show involves temperament. A show cat must be well socialized and comfortable when handled by strangers. Your Tonkinese should be accustomed to the loud noises she may confront in the show hall. Introducing your cat to the type of examination performed by the judges is important. Watch how the judges handle the cats at a few cat shows

and then go through the same motions with your cat at home.

The Judging

When you arrive at the show, you will check in at the front door. A quick examination by a veterinarian may be given to make sure that your cat will not pose a health threat to other cats. The "vet check" is almost unheard of at shows in the US, but it is common in other countries. You will be given a catalog describing each cat in the

It's smart to attend a few shows before attempting to show your cat for the first time. Make sure to find some other friendly Tonkinese fanciers and introduce yourself. *Photo: Lorraine Shelton*

show and a number to place on the cage to identify your cat. You will also be assigned a place to cage your cat.

In some associations, you must leave the show hall while the judge and the steward handle your cat for judging. Your cage cannot identify you or your cat in any way other than the number assigned him at that show. Results are posted and awards assigned, and then you are permitted to return to the show hall. The show will then be opened to the public, and you may decorate your cage for exhibition.

In other associations, and in all shows in the US, you are permitted to decorate your show cage, and you will stay with your cat for the entire show day. When it is time for your cat to be judged, her number will be called. You will then bring her to the judging ring and place her in another cage with her number on top. When judging has concluded and awards (usually flat ribbons) within a breed have been distributed, your cat will be dismissed and you will bring her back to her benching cage. After handling all cats of a particular group (Kittens, Shorthaired Cats, or All-Breed Alters, for example), the judge will ask for some cats to return to the ring so that they may be presented with the top prizes, usually rosettes. This

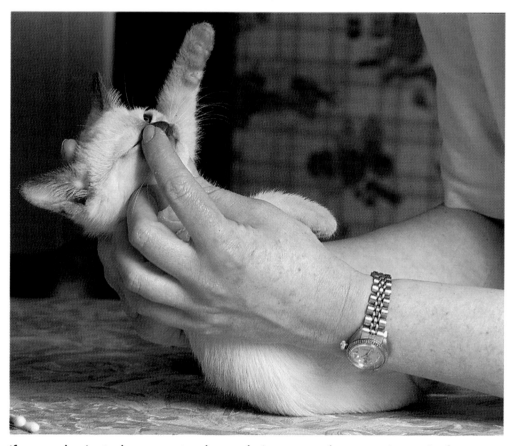

If you are planning to show your cat, make sure she is accustomed to a grooming routine from a very young age. *Photo: Isabelle Francais*

THE GUIDE TO OWNING A TONKINESE CAT

Whether or not your cat returns home from the show with a bouquet of satin rosettes, your first show will be an unforgettable experience. *Photo: Lorraine Shelton*

In all shows in the US, exhibitors are permitted to decorate the show cage, and many create lavish setups for their cats. *Photo: Karen White*

portion of the show is called the Final. Each judge will present finals in each category that she has been assigned to judge, whether All-Breed (the top cats regardless of breed) or Specialty (only short-haired cats, only Tonkinese cats, etc.).

Each judge comprises his or her own independent cat show, although at the end of all judging, the placings may be tallied to determine Best in Show, which is awarded in a separate ceremony. In other shows, a separate judging will be held among the top winning cats of the show to determine Best in Show. This will be presided over by a judge or panel of judges that have not handled the cats earlier in the weekend.

Whether or not your cat returns home from the show with a bouquet of satin rosettes, you will have had a day (or weekend) full of camaraderie with fellow cat lovers. You will return more educated about your breed, and your cat will have encountered those special people who have dedicated their lives to the admiration of the beauty of cats: cat show judges.

Cat Registry Associations

**American Association
of Cat Enthusiasts**
P.O. Box 213
Pine Brook, NJ 07058
Phone: 973-335-6717
Fax: 973-334-5834
E-mail: info@aaceinc.org
Web: www.aaceinc.org/
welcome.html

American Cat Fanciers Association
P.O. Box 203
Point Lookout, MO 65726
Phone: 417-334-5430
Fax: 417-334-5540
E-mail: info@acfacat.com
Web: acfacat.com

Australian Cat Federation (Inc)
Post Office Box 3305
Port Adelaide SA 5015
Phone: 08 8449 5880
Fax: 08 8242 2767
E-mail: acf@catlover.com
Web: www.acf.asn.au

Canadian Cat Association
220 Advance Blvd,
Suite 101
Brampton, Ontario
Canada L6T 4J5
Phone: 905-459-1481
Fax: 905-459-4023
E-mail: office@cca-afc.com
Web: www.cca-afc.com

The Cat Fanciers' Association, Inc.
P.O. Box 1005
Manasquan, NJ 08736-0805
Phone: 732-528-9797
Fax: 732-528-7391
E-mail: cfa@cfainc.org
Web: www.cfainc.org

Cat Fanciers Federation
P.O. Box 661
Gratis, OH 45330
Phone: 937-787-9009
Fax: 937-787-4290
E-mail: cff@siscom.net
Web: www.cffinc.org

**Cat Federation
of Southern Africa**
P.O. Box 25
Bromhof 2125
Rep. of South Africa
Phone or Fax: +27 11 867-4318
E-mail: webmaster@ cfsa.co.za
Web: www.cfsa.co.za

Federation Internationale Feline
Ms. Penelope Bydlinski
Little Dene
Lenham Heath
Maidstone, Kent
GB-ME17 2BS
Phone: +44 1622 850913
Fax: +44 1622 850908
E-mail: penbyd@ compuserve.com
Web: www.fife.org

**Federazione Italiana Associazioni
Feline**
c/o Rag. Cesare Ghisi
Via Carlo Poma n.20
46100—Mantova, Italy
Phone: 0376-224600
Fax: 0376-224041
E-mail: fiafmn@mynet.it
Web: www.zero.it/fiaf

**The Feline Control
Council of Victoria, Inc.**
Royal Melbourne Showgrounds
Epsom Road, Ascot Vale,
Victoria 3032, Australia
Phone: (03) 9281 7404
Fax: (03) 9376 2973
E-mail: m.jones@ rasv.metbourne.net
Web: www.hotkey.net.au/ ~fccvic

**Governing Council
of the Cat Fancy**
4-6 Penel Orlieu
Bridgwater, Somerset,
TA6 3PG. (UK)
Phone: +44 (0) 1278 427 575
E-mail: GCCF_CATS@compuserve.com
Web: ourworld. compuserve.com/
homepages/GCCF_CATS/
welcome.htm#office

**International
Cat Exhibitors, Inc.**
P.O. Box 772424
Coral Springs, FL 33077-2424
Web: members.aol.com/
jhagercat/ICE.htm

The International Cat Association, Inc.
P.O. Box 2684
Harlingen, TX 78551
Phone: 956-428-8047
Fax: 956-428-8047
E-mail: ticaeoe@ xanadu2.net
Web: www.tica.org

United Feline Organization
218 NW 180th Street
Newberry, FL 32669
Phone and Fax: 352-472-3253
Email: UFO1FL@ worldnet.att.net
Web: www.aracnet.com/ ~ltdltd/
ufo.htm

World Cat Federation
Hubertstraße 280
D-45307 Essen, Germany
Phone: +49 201/555724
Fax: +49 201/509040
E-mail: wcf@nrw-online.de
Web: home.nrw-online.de/wcf/
english/ehome.html

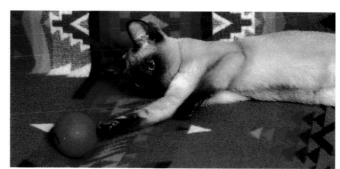

Index